G. W McGrew

The Story of a Bell

And Other Poems

G. W McGrew

The Story of a Bell
And Other Poems

ISBN/EAN: 9783744652278

Printed in Europe, USA, Canada, Australia, Japan

Cover: Foto ©Thomas Meinert / pixelio.de

More available books at **www.hansebooks.com**

THE

STORY OF A BELL

AND

OTHER POEMS.

— BY —

G. W. McGREW,

SARATOGA, CAL.

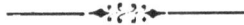

SAN JOSE, CAL.:
TIMES-MERCURY STEAM BOOK AND JOB PRINT.
1885.

CONTENTS.

PART I.*

SITTING at my chamber window,
  Basking in the sunbeams bright,
Comes there through the open casement,
  On the south wind soft and light,
Mellow notes of distant music,
  As the zephyrs rise and swell,
And my heart throbs as I listen
  To the music of my bell.

Would you know why thus I call it?
  Why to me it is so dear?
Well, just take a seat beside me,
  And my story you shall hear.
On the porch, if you prefer it,
  And will help to move my chair;
There we'll get God's blessed sunshine,
  And the fresh, sweet morning air.

But you must have stores of patience,
  For my story may be long,
For, you see, I'm old and feeble,
  And my brain no longer strong,
And, besides, it may be simple,
  With but little thought or care—
Childish as a nursery story,
  Or an infant's evening prayer.

* Written in March, 1885.

When the sands of life grow scanty,
　And the stream flows weak and low,
And the heart again grows childish
　'Neath the almond's wintry blow,
We may ask and claim some freedom
　From exacting rules of life,
Or, at least, may make such pretext,
　To escape the critic's knife.

We were living then at Larkland—
　When?　About four years ago—
That lies northward from Los Gatos
　Just about a mile or so.
There we built a modest cottage,
　Hoping yet to make a home;
But, alas, the same old story—
　Got a mortgage for a dome.

How we toiled, and prayed, and struggled,
　In suspense 'twixt hope and fear,
Might form subject for a chapter,
　But can have no presence here.
One day, feeling rather lonesome,
　I set out to find a man,
Said to be a fellow churchman—
　All the one in all that land.

For our neighbors then were strangers,
　In the region where we dwelt,
For the climate was so lovely—

It was called the great warm belt—
  It drew many from the cities
    Down about the Golden Gate,
And the weary health-home seekers
    From each chilly Northern State.

Found my man out in the garden,
    Busy with his hoe and rake.
When I told him all my errand,
    Smiling, said, "There's some mistake;
I'm a Baptist," said he, leaning
    On the handle of his hoe.
"If you're hunting Presbyterians
    I can tell you where to go."

Well he told me, and I found them
    At their cottage on the hill,
Loyal, loving, Christian people—
    Would that they were with us still;
But like pilgrims on a journey,
    We can tarry but a night—
Meet to love, then part assunder
    Till the dawn of heavenly light.

Other kindred hearts were added,
    And the little circle grew,
No one knowing as they gathered
    Why their love grew strong and true.
From this tiny seed of mustard,

Scarce observed by human eyes,
Nurtured by the dews of heaven,
Lo! we see a church arise.

Not without consideration,
And much thoughtful, anxious care,
Lest some hasty step be taken,
But with fervent, earnest prayer
That the King who reigns in Zion,
Far above all human sight,
Would enlighten by His spirit
And direct our steps aright.

PART II.*

'TWAS a little band of pilgrims,
Whose hearts the Lord impressed
With a wish to walk together
To the country of the blest.
Some lived upon the mountain side,
Some down upon the plain,
And some in the pretty village
Midway between the twain.

But their hearts were drawn together
With cords of love divine,
Just as the Master promised when
He left the world behind.

* Written in June, 1884, and published as an "Anniversary Poem."

So they loved to talk together,
  As they journeyed on the way,
Of the glorious heavenly prospects
  That just before them lay.

But, like sheep without a shepherd,
  Or like lambs without a fold,
This little band of pilgrims
  Were scattered in the cold.
For this world of sin and sorrow,
  Though like an Eden dressed,
Is not the land of Canaan,
  Where weary pilgrims rest.

So they prayed to have a shepherd,
  To lead them on the way,
By the quiet crystal waters,
  Where greenest pastures lay.
And a fold enclosed securely,
  Where weary feet might rest,
And a place for sweet communion
  With friends they loved the best.

Now just how this prayer was answered,
  I'll tell, if you would know,
For it happened in Los Gatos,
  About three years ago.
First of all, to drop the figure,
  These were men, like you and me,

And it was a church they wanted,
   Not a fold, as you shall see.

And a preacher for a shepherd—
   Though I like that name the best —
But no difference, so he leads us
   In the footsteps of the blessed.
So, one day, when met together, *
   In a rather spacious hall,
Though they did not try to fill it—
   Just one corner, that was all—

When the call was made for members,
   Twenty-three rose to their feet.
So the little church was started —
   Small, but organized complete.
Not so briefly as I've told you
   Were the services that day,
But the form was short and simple,
   So I heard some people say.

Now, while they're waiting in the hall,
   With half an answered prayer,
Just come with me, on Fancy's wing,
   Up through the Eastern air.
We pause not in our magic flight,
   Almost from sea to sea,
Till stern New England's sternest State
   Is reached by you and me.

---

* The Church was organized by Rev. J. M. Newell, July 3, 1881.

On bold Mount Mansfield's rocky crest,
　　We pause awhile to scan
The glory of Green Mountain scenes
　　Spread out on every hand.
Huge fir-clad hills, rock-ribbed and wild,
　　Whose every clifted glen
Reveals some glimpse of mountain homes—
　　Fit homes for stalwart men.

Hills sloping downward to the vale,
　　With many a leafy dell,
Whose hidden springs, cool babbling brooks
　　Their hiding places tell.
Green pasture lands, small, well-kept farms,
　　Bright thrift on every side;
The church, the school, the busy mill,
　　New England's boast and pride.

From out such scenes one sweet June day,
　　There came a wedded pair;
I know not how it came about,
　　Nor need you know or care.
He, the young preacher, just from school,
　　With proof enough at hand,
And she, the maiden of his choice—
　　So let that matter stand.

I do not like to say farewell
　　To home and kindred dear;
We'll skip the parting, you and I,

Without one single tear,
When seated in the flying train,
  The preacher and his bride,
Methinks I almost hear him say,
  " Now for that promised ride."

That day, for which they toiled and prayed,
  Through years of hope deferred,
Had dawned at last upon the earth,
  And all their prayers were heard.
With strong young hearts of faith and love,
  Inspired to burning zeal,
They blessed the speed that winged them on
  To their far western field.

Like one of old who left his home
  And kin at God's command,
They knew not where their lot might be
  In that broad western land;
But He who calls a willing heart,
  And fills it with His grace,
And qualifies for special work,
  Will help to find the place.

'Twas by no accident or chance,
  As we sat waiting there,
A stranger came,* and by his side
  A youthful lady fair.

---

* Rev. R. C. Moodie supplied the pulpit from the day the church was organized. He was ordained and installed Nov. 8, 1881.

We knew not then, nor did they know,
  As we both know to-day,
Their coming answered all our prayer,
  How glad! They came to stay.

Since that, to us, eventful day,
  Three years have passed in peace;
The Lord has crowned our feeble work
  With comforting increase.
The little band of twenty-three
  We count by scores to-day;
Three score and ten are on the roll,
  And some have moved away.

One precious name we cherish still,
  Though it is claimed above;
Death can not break the golden chain,
  The bond of Christian love. †
Like some sweet flower, plucked at noon,
  And carried to the skies,
We miss the form, but in our hearts
  The fragrance never dies.

With grateful hearts we look to-day
  Back to our infant days,
When we were few, and weak and poor,
  And little knew the ways
A church could rise from such small means

† Mrs. W. W. Dull died June 28, 1883.

And all its wants be fed;
But we had faith in barley loaves
When Jesus breaks the bread.

The pioneer must build a tent
A chapel it may be—
While Hiram gets the cedars out
And brings them by the sea.
A house to serve the future years,
Costs time as well as gold-
It took the wise man seven years
To build his house, we're told.

Our little chapel we've outgrown;
It served our purpose well.
Now friends if you will build the church,
I'll try to raise the bell,
Whose every note may be a call
To him who came to save,
" When this poor, lisping, stammering tongue
Lies silent in the grave."

PART III.*

ALL the long bright days of summer
My poor bark was ill at ease;
Like the ebb and flow of ocean,
I had wrestled with disease.

* Written in March, 1885.

Sometimes out among the sunbeams,
  Tasting sweetness in the air;
Sometimes plunged beneath the shadows
  With no comfort anywhere.

When the summer days grew shorter
  Autumn came with sober mien,
With its wealth of golden sunshine,
  Ripening fruit and waving grain;
But to me it brought no healing,
  As I drooped from place to place,
Seeking strength, but finding weakness,
  While worse symptoms grew apace.

All these days of cloud and sunshine
  On my heart a burden lay,
Sometimes light and sometimes heavy,
  With the light and shadows play.
In my zeal to aid my brethren,
  And the sacred cause as well,
I had made a hasty promise
  That I'd try to raise a bell.

Was it rashness or presumption
  Prompting this bold word to speak,
Since I knew my purse was empty,
  And, perhaps, my credit weak.
Yet, somehow, this new dilemma
  Brought more happiness than pain,

So I set myself to planning
    How to make all right again.

I was now a weary prisoner
    In my chamber neat and bright
Two large windows to the southward
    For the noontide's sun and light.
One looked eastward to the rising,
    One toward the setting sun,
And what loving hearts could bring me
    Was, I knew, most gladly done.

Sometimes, when the sun was brightest,
    And my brain was brightest too,
With my paper in the sunshine
    I could sit to write a few
Crooked lines I called my letters
    To my friends both east and west,
Telling all about my interest
    In the church I loved the best.

Oh, the charm of human friendship,
    Christian sympathy and love;
How it lightens all our burdens
    With a joy like that above.
Struggling through my pain and blindness,
    Bungling work I made that way,
But kind answers came beguiling
    Many a long and weary day.

Still, to aid me in my effort,
  I enclosed a simple rhyme
I had written for our people
  At their last good annual time.
Though the hand was weak and trembling,
  And the harp unstrung and wrong,
Some sweet chord brought quick responses
  To the burden of my song.

Northward, far as Walla Walla,
  Came the messages of love;
Southward, from the "Angel city,"
  Nestled in her orange grove;
Eastward, from the broad Atlantic,
  From the rugged coast of Maine—
From the mountains and the valleys,
  And the cities of the plain.

Far across the broad Pacific,
  Far beyond the tropic's land,
From another Mount of Olives,
  Looking o'er New Zealand's strand;
From a home near Auckland City,
  Looking out upon the sea,
Came a letter richly freighted
  With good words of cheer for me.

Not kinds words alone, but money,
  Proving sympathy sincere—

Timely aid in my dilemma,
    How to keep my conscience clear.
Bells are bells, and cost much money—
    Where to find it who could tell?
Did you ever hear such story—
    How a poor man raised a bell?

Now the pretty foothill beauty
    Adds a jewel to her crown—
Upward points another steeple,
    Calling Heaven's blessings down;
And well poised up in the belfry
    Hangs my sweet-tongued Blymyer bell,
May it hang and ring for ages,
    No uncertain sound to tell.

Now the pleasant task is finished,
    Now the burden's laid aside—
Thanks to Thee, O, God, the Giver,
    For the strength Thy grace supplied.
May Thy blessing rest upon it,
    And on all who placed it there;
And on all who hear and heed it
    While it calls to praise and prayer.

Dedicatory Hymn.

TUNE—*Asmon.* *

ALMIGHTY God, each heart inspire
   With gratitude and love,
That all our songs of praise this day
   May be like those above.

We come with grateful hearts to bring
   A tribute to Thy shrine,
Though all we have to give or keep
   Most sacredly is Thine.

The trees grew on the mountain slopes
   Fanned by the western sea;
And all the goodness of the house
   We gladly trace to Thee.

Though Heaven itself cannot contain
   Thy glory and Thy grace,
In wondrous condescension make
   This house Thy dwelling place.

It is the gift of many hearts,
   The work of many hands;
It is the child of many prayers.
   Accept it as it stands.

* Sung at the dedication of the church, May 3, 1885.

Here let Thy name recorded be,
And when Thy children meet
To worship in this sacred place,
O make Thy presence sweet!

When here Thy servant stands between
The living and the dead;
Clothe Thine own word with power divine,
That all Thy saints be fed;

That from these courts a stream may flow,
To gladden all the land,
And many weary wandering feet,
Be turned to Thy right hand.

Los Gatos.

THERE'S a cosy little village, *
    Half hidden in the woods,
Where the murmuring Los Gatos,
    Pours down its crystal floods
Through the wild and rocky canyon
    That cleaves the mountain high,
That bounds the fairest valley
    Beneath our western sky.

This lovely little village
    Hath charms beyond compare,
Of wild, romantic beauty,
    And cultured gardens fair;
For herethe wooded mountains,
    The valley orchards meet,
And the oak trees and the orange
    Shake hands across the street.

There's an air of careless beauty,
    That runs through all the town;
The streets go rambling where they please,
    With sidewalks up and down;
Some homes have found a level spot,
    To put on city airs,

* Written in June, 1881.

While others peep from shady heights,
　Above a flight of stairs.

There are views of matchless beauty,
　From every cottage door;
The mountains! O, the mountains!
　And the valley's painted floor,
Bedecked with homes and hamlets, as
　It northward fades away,
Till its wheat fields, groves and gardens,
　Kiss the waters of the bay.

Far up across the canyon,
　O'er the summit bold and high,
There's a fringe of noble redwoods
　Against the western sky;
While far eastward, o'er the valley,
　Mount Hamilton is seen,
With the Garden City nestling
　In the lovely vale between.

But for scenes of rarest beauty,
　You need not look away
To the distant chain of mountains
　That circles half the bay;
Nor yet to the lofty summit
　That overlooks the sea,
That casts its evening shadow
　Across our little lea.

Nor yet to the quiet valley
   That lies beneath your feet,
With its fruitful groves and gardens,
   And fields of golden wheat;
There are gems of rural beauty
   Just round about the town,
So pretty, that you think each one
   The loveliest you have found.

You see them as you walk the street,
   You see them from the hill,
You see them as you cross the bridge
   Above the old stone mill—
You see them morning, noon, and eve,
   In every changing light,
But oh! how picturesquely!
   When luna crowns the night.

But this modest little village
   By the babbling water's brink,
Is not so dull and idle
   As a passer-by might think;
There's quite a stir of business
   In the narrow, crooked street,
Where the traffic of the mountains
   And the valley traders meet.

Huge loads of wood and lumber
   Come lumbering down the grade;
While the flying train goes flashing

Through the sunshine and the shade;
A hum of wheels in motion
  Comes up from the old stone mill,
All hoary with age and flour,
  As it grinds and grinds on still.

That burst of merry voices
  That rings out on the breeze,
Comes out from the village school-house,
  Hid somewhere 'mong the trees;
Six days the anvil chorus
  Rings out upon the air,
On Sabbath morn one single bell
  Calls sweetly out to prayer.

Of all religions it is said,
  (I mention what I read)
The altar and the temple both,
  Do shadow forth the creed;
But the people of this village,
  (To lay aside all jokes,)
Are not a set of Druids,
  Though they worship under oaks.

O, lovely, rustic beauty!
  With all thy simple ways,
Let not the tyrant Fashion
  Cut short thy happy days;
Preserve with stern devotion
  The beauty God has given;
'Twill help to sweeten earthly toil
  And point the road to Heaven.

Thirty-fifth Wedding Anniversary.

DEAR wife, 'tis five and thirty years
    Since you and I were wed;
It seems not half so long to me,
    Time has so lightly sped.
Though all our way has not been smooth,
    Our day not always bright,
Yet God has tinged our darkest clouds
    With His own loving light.

Most of the friends that 'round us stood
    That lovely April day
To hear our vows and wish us joy
    From earth have passed away.
But nearer still Death's shadows came,
    As we passed down the years—
Four little graves, laid far apart,
    Have witness borne of tears.

One after one our cherished plans
    Of home and plenty crowned
Have met misfortune's blighting touch
    And fallen to the ground.
And yet, somehow, we've got along,
    Despite our useless fears,

For God has led us side by side
These five and thirty years.

What though we've had some stormy days
  Our hearts are happy still,
For surely in the checkered past
  We've had more good than ill.
So, not one mournful chord I'll touch
  To mar our joy to-day,
For light, you know, is doubly sweet
  As darkness rolls away.

While struggling through life's toilsome way,
  It oft has grieved my heart
That one endowed with gifts so rare
  Should share so dull a part;
But genius ne'er can be suppressed,
  Though humble be thy lot;
Such taste as thine can almost make
  A palace of a cot.

Thus, while we've drifted, here and there,
  With fortunes good or bad,
'Twas thine to cheer the way and make
  The best of what we had;
And well, my dear, thou'st done thy part
  In every trying day,
With patience, love, and taste combined,
  To smooth life's rugged way.

To bear each other's griefs and cares
  Has made our burdens light;
To share each others happiness
  Has made our joys more bright.
Not all the sweetest flowers of earth
  Are born of cloudless skies;
Full many a gem of clouded birth
  Shall bloom in paradise.

The sweetest lesson we have learned,
  And yet are learning still,
Is just to leave it all with God,
  And have no other will;
Accept the mission of our lives,
  Our prayer, as it is sent,
" Give us this day our daily bread,"
  And therewith be content.

But Time, my dear, is on the wing,
  Nor would we stay his flight;
The shades of time will soon be lost
  In God's eternal light;
Then, as we stand before His face,
  O, will it not seem good,
To hear the Master say, again,
  " She hath done what she could."

Twilight Musing.

THE toil of the day was ended,
   And I turned for a little rest,
But a feeling of sadness lingered,
   Like a pall o'er my weary breast;
The thought that my lot was a hard one
   Came up, but I turned it aside,
While I groped in the dark for the promise
   That in some way the Lord would provide.

With burdens so great and so many,
   And the strength of a broken reed,
I asked, in my anguish of spirit,
   O, how can a mortal succeed?
I knew that to groan was not manly,
   To distrust, I knew was a sin,
Yet still the dark billow came o'er me
   With naught to resist it within.

O'erwhelmed with a sense of my weakness,
   I ventured to lift up my eyes,
Through the mist that was gathering o'er them
   To the glorious light of the skies.
The sun had passed over the summit,
   That stands by the western main,

The foothills, all draped in shadows,
   Stretched out like a veil t'ward the plain.

The mountains encircling the valley,
   Enrobed in their purple and blue,
Proclaimed as of old the sweet promise,
   That God to His people is true.
''His righteousness like the great mountains,''
   Came down, as it seemed, from the hight
Where the last ray of daylight lingers,
   And the dawning first heralds the light.

In silence I gazed at the wonders
   Displayed by the changing light,
As the earth beneath grew darker,
   And the Heavens above more bright,
Till filled by the inspiration,
   As upward it bore me along,
The pall from my heart was lifted,
   And my groaning was turned to a song.

Los Gatos, Cal., Nov. 5, 1881.

Going Blind.

THE world is fading from my sight—
   Slow, but surely away—
And all that God has made so bright
   Grows dimmer every day.
Not but the fields are just as green,
   The sky above as blue,
The dimness comes to me alone,
   From the veil I see them through.

This veil—the trace of pain and years
   On this poor throbbing brain—
Shuts out the beauty of the world,
   Letting its shades remain.
The smiles and frowns of friends and foes
   Are all the same to me—
I miss their pleasure and their pain
   Because I cannot see.

Thus, blundering on my lonesome way,
   Though in a crowded street,
I scarce can tell my dearest friends
   From strangers whom I meet.
Yet, in the busy fray of life
   I still must hold a place—

The doom from Eden yet enthralls
  The toilers of our race.

Patience, O, weary, troubled heart,
  The race will soon be run;
The shadows gath'ring o'er thy path
  Foretell a brighter sun.
Though all the earth grows poor and dark
  The eye of faith grows bright;
God is the portion of thy heart—
  Thine everlasting light.

Los Gatos, Cal., Jan. 1, 1883.

Our Old Oak Tree.

ABOUT a thousand years ago,
 It might be hundreds less,
For when we can not know a thing
 We only have to guess;
A tiny acorn rattled down
 From some old tree that stood,
About a thousand years ago,
 The monarch of this wood.

The tiny acorn rattled down
 As soft the south wind blew,
To find a leafy hiding place,
 From which this old oak grew.
But how it grew, or why it grew,
 So crooked, rough, and low,
It has no tongue, and who can tell
 What happened long ago?

While seated 'neath thy shade, old tree,
 Upon my rustic chair,
The sea breeze rustling through thy leaves
 Lifting my silvered hair,
I've wondered what thy past could tell,
 If such a thing might be,

To weave a sympathetic chord
  Between myself and thee.

Thy low bent trunk, deep scarred and gnarled,
  Bears record of the past,
Of crushing harm from other trees,
  Or tempests' fearful blast,
Scat'ring thy beauty to the winds
  Like leaves before the gale,
·Leaving a living monument
  To tell its own sad tale.

Thus robbed of beauty, form and grace,
  With sprawling head bent low,
Thy very worthlessness has saved
  Thee from the axman's blow;
No woodman ever thought thee harm,
  So thou hast held the field;
Not one straight stick of four-foot wood
  Thy crooked top would yield.

But naught, 'tis said, was made in vain,
  I hope the doctrine true;
Some grains of comfort it might bring
  To me as well as you,
Despoiled of beauty, not of life,
  A mission thou wast given;
Some humble link in that great chain
  Which binds all earth to Heaven.

Was it with every passing breeze
    To sound His praise abroad,
To point the sluggish heart of man
    Through nature up to God?
To welcome spring with buds and bloom,
    And summer with her sheaves;
To deck the graves of parting years
    With wreaths of russet leaves?

To welcome to thy cooling shade,
    Through all the summer days,
The meadow lark, thy constant friend,
    With all his merry lays?
To welcome to thy heart of oak,
    With gnarly hands outspread,
The living things that God has made,
    To shelter, board and bed?

'Twas but last summer, one fair day,
    A wandering swarm of bees
Came swooping down to thy low top,
    Past groves of finer trees;
In thy low, rough, unsightly trunk,
    To find an open door,
Where scores of squirrels had raised thei.
        broods,
Five hundred years before.

Ah! yes, old tree, a mission thine,
    I see it now more clear;

A lesson, too, it brings to me,
  I have been slow to hear—
That scrubby trees should be content,
  And faulty men as well,
To take what comes, and fill their niche,
  And try to do it well.

Los Gatos, Cal., Mar. 17th, 1883.

The Autumn Time Has Come.

JUST merging from the gloomy vale
   That timid mortals dread—
Down by the gate that stands between
   The living and the dead—
God's sunshine falls upon my heart
   With new and strange delight,
Because the time has been so long
   Since I enjoyed its light.

When last I saw the outside world,
   And breathed the fragrant air,
The fields were dressed in living green,
   And all the world was fair.
Now from my chamber window, where
   A prisoner I remain,
I see the autumn time has come,
   With all its sober train.

The hills and dales have doffed the green
   For autumn's russet gray,
And stubble fields look brown and bare,
   And dusty as the way—
The broad highway that leads to town,
   Traced by the dusty train,

That follows every whirling wheel,
  O'er valley, hill and plain.

The sturdy oaks that spread their limbs
  Above the cottage eaves,
Moan sadly as the autumn winds
  Strip off their withered leaves.
The orchard trees look poor and thin,
  As picking time goes by,
And long-bent limbs find sweet relief
  Against the azure sky.

The vineyard, too, has been despoiled
  Of summer's clustered gain;
While tangled vines and faded leaves
  Are all that now remain.
The luscious grapes of many hues,
  That ripened here of late,
Have found a passage to the East,
  Or to the Golden Gate.

The little bird that hailed the dawn
  With carols low and sweet
Has left its haunts about the house,
  A restless band to meet
Of kindred birds that soar away,
  Then back again at night,
As if to test their little wings
  For some extended flight.

O'er all the landscape far and near,
  Up to the mountain's crest,
A dreamy haze pervades the air,
  Suggestive of the rest
A kindly nature grants to all
  Within her broad domain —
A rest, a sleep, a death, a grave,
  Till they shall rise again.

Yes, while I at the window sit,
  In weakness and in pain,
To see the autumn time has come,
  With all its sober train,
Responsive from my heart there comes
  A note of sympathy;
I, too, am in the yellow leaf —
  Autumn has come to me.

I feel it in my trembling frame,
  And in my failing sight,
And in my treach'rous memory,
  That fails me as I write.
I feel it as I long for rest,
  Beyond all mortal care —
My yearning for some unknown good
  That seeks relief in prayer.

Great God of nature and of grace,
  I would look up to Thee,

I know my times are in Thy hand,
    And all my destiny.
Keep this declining life of mine
    In Thine Almighty hand,
Then I shall triumph over death,
    And reach the better land.

＊

BOWDISH RANCH, Los Gatos, Cal., Oct., 188?.

To My Wife.

While detained by business in Cincinnati, in the fall of 1848, I wrote
the following lines to my wife on the back of one of my first business
cards. I was agreeably surprised to learn, not long since, that she had
carefully preserved this card among her sacred relics.

I AM weary, O, how weary,
    Of the city's dust and din.
 Would that I could fly and leave it
    In its folly, noise and sin,
For my own loved little cottage---
    For my own bright fireside---
And the one on earth the dearest---
    Heaven's gift---my wife, my bride.

Set Aside.

YES, just as well be set aside,
  The world moves all the same,
Suns rise and set, moons wax and wane,
  Regardless of my name—
Whether I take an active part
  In all beneath the sun,
Or fold my hands and step aside
  And say my work is done.

The country, too, goes on as if
  It might sustain the shock;
The ship of state glides smoothly on
  Without a reef or rock;
The State elections come and go
  Without my casting voice;
They make and unmake presidents
  Regardless of my choice.

The world of business surges on
  Along the lines of trade,
And stocks go up and stocks go down
  Without my ken or aid.
No city merchant cares to know
  My standing at the banks;

No board of traders, high or low,
　　Now miss me from their ranks.

Then in the church—my chosen field
　　Of labor and delight,
Where once, no doubt, I thought myself
　　A pillar and a light—
They manage somehow to get on
　　Without my sage advice—
Indeed I fear they scarcely miss
　　Me from their councils wise.

My place so near the pulpit step,
　　That not a word might slip,
To get the blessed gospel news
　　Warm from the pastor's lip,
Has been so long by others filled
　　My claim has passed away;
I'm glad that in the upper church
　　They go not out for aye.

Then in the home, that sacred spot,
　　The last stronghold of life,
My ruling star is on the wane—
　　I'm boarding with my wife.
On stormy days I stay within,
　　And lounge about at ease;
When warm and fine I court the sun,
　　Or sit beneath the trees.

I take no hand at work or play,
   I seldom read or write.
I'm tired, and I rest all day,
   Then try to rest at night.
Sometimes I ask at evening tide,
   What have I done to-day?
The answer comes, with some regret—
   I've passed the time away.

Ah, yes! I see I'm set aside,
   I feel it every day,
The world, the church, the social ring,
   The sober and the gay,
They pass me by without concern,
   I'm satisfied 'tis so,
Yet with my joy there's some regret
   That I am letting go.

SARATOGA, Cal., March 1, 1881.

Three Score and Ten.

MY three score years and ten. How strange!
   I note it down with care;
I never thought to live so long,
   Nor was it in my prayer.
But God is good and kind and wise,
   And doeth all things well;
But why this life should be so long,
   I think, but can not tell.

If I were well, and strong, and wise,
   And qualified to stand
Among the rulers of the state,
   Or tillers of the land,
Or be a leader in some scheme
   To benefit the race,
I then might better understand
   Why I should have a place.

But this poor, weary, idle life,
   So near to death akin,
Almost as helpless as a child,
   Without its charms to win;
So long the care of anxious hearts,
   And overburdened hands,

With naught to recompense but love,
　　As gratitude demands.

But God is good, and kind and wise,
　　And doeth all things well.
We may not understand His ways,
　　Nor all His wonders tell,
But we may trust Him for His grace,
　　Whose mercies are so great;
For they, 'tis said, do also serve,
　　Who only stand and wait.

Some humble mission yet may be,
　　My portion as I wait;
The grace of patience it may be,
　　How best to illustrate.
In my own life, that all may see,
　　The power of grace divine,
To cheer and comfort with the faith,
　　That smiles at life's decline.

Great God, possess this truant heart,
　　And mould it to Thy will,
That this poor fragment of a life,
　　Be Thine more fully still.
If through this vale Thy rod and staff
　　But keep me in the way,
There shall be light at evening-time,
　　More perfect than the day.

SARATOGA, CAL., March 29, 1885.

On the Banks of Boulder.

Boulder City, Colorado, is situated near the mouth of the famous Boulder Canyon, through which Boulder Creek tumbles and foams down from the snowy range to the plains on which the city stands. The road up this canyon from Boulder to the mining town of Caribou, a distance of 22 miles, is considered one of the wildest and most picturesque the Rocky Mountains, and one which no tourist should fail to see. While resting one warm day on some rocks under a willow on the banks of the stream I perpetrated the following impromptu lines:

N the banks of Boulder,
A rock to rest my shoulder,
I'll sit till I am older,
    A minute—maybe two;

To hear the waters prattle,
To hear them roar and rattle,
As on they dash in battle,
    'Gainst rocks, in passing through.

I'd like to stay some longer,
If I were young and stronger,
Or if my time was longer—
    But I must bid adieu.

I'd like to find the fountain,
Away up in the mountain,
That sends these waters flountin'
    Adown from Caribou.

Aug. 18, 1877.

Lines Written in a Lady's Album.

WHAT is a name? a single word,
  That word we love most dear!
We love ourselves, we love our names,
  We write them everywhere.

Deep rooted in the human heart,
  Perhaps it is divine
The principle which makes us wish
  To leave our names behind.

Like flowers that bloom in early spring,
  That bloom but for a day,
So we are passing one by one—
  We live and pass away.

As travelers to some distant clime,
  Far over life's rough sea;
We leave our mottoes here behind—
  Those mottoes are, " Remember me."

'Tis this that wings the poets' flight,
  O'er fancy's field to roam;
'Tis this that nerves the warrior arms
  To strike for friends and home.

We carve them in the solid rock,
  We mark them on the ground,

We cut them on the forest tree,
　We see them all around.

And lady, in this book of thine,
　There's many a cherished name;
I know them not, but yet I know
　Their object was the same.

Scattered like jewels through thy book,
　They these inscriptions gave,
That in thy memory they might dwell,
　No greater boon I crave.

But, oh! how vain, how vain the thought,
　To cheat Time of his prey;
No monument that we can raise
　But Time will sweep away.

Fame, wealth, and honor are but sounds,
　That soon will die away;
Rocks, trees, and books, and marble urns,
　Are creatures of decay.

One book alone shall stand secure,
　When Time has ceased his strife –
High in the library of Heaven--
　It is the Book of Life.

Oh! lady, may thy name and mine,
　And all the names recorded here,
When this, and all earth's books are lost,
　In the Lamb's Book of Life appear.

SIDNEY, Ohio, 1846.

My Sister's Grave.

MY sister's grave, my sister's grave,
　　How lone and still it lies
In the quiet village churchyard,
　　Beneath the bending skies.
Exposed to wind and tempest,
　　Without a tree to save,
The sunshine and the shower
　　Fall on my sister's grave.

Ah, well do I remember,
　　Can I forget the scene?
In early spring we made it,
　　Before the earth was green.
We gathered all around it,
　　Our last adieu we gave,
And many bitter tears we shed
　　Upon my sister's grave.

Through all the months of summer
　　I've watched the hallowed spot,
And on the Sabbath evening
　　Its sacredness I've sought,
But not with drops of sorrow
　　Its long green grass to lave;

My nearest views of Heaven
    Were from my sister's grave.

Now the chilly winds of autumn
    Moan sadly as they sweep
Where the quiet dead are resting,
    Unconscious in their sleep,
That early frosts have blighted
    The covering nature gave;
. But spring will come with beauty
    To deck my sister's grave.

The loved one that here lieth,
    But not in endless sleep,
Shall, like the blighted flowers
    That o'er her bosom weep,
Arise in heavenly beauty,
    Through Him who came to save,
'Tis this that sheds such glory
    Around my sister's grave.

SIDNEY, Ohio, Nov., 1845.

Parting Words.

Written when increasing pains seemed to suggest that the end was near. May, 1885.

COME, my wife, sit close beside me,
   I would feel thy presence, dear;
For who knows what may betide me,
   When the end is drawing near.
I may lose my speech and reason,
   If the fever rages high,
And, perhaps, might fail to tell thee
   What I wish before I die.

Thanks to Thee, O, Heavenly Father,
   For these intervals of rest—
Precious hours of sweet communing
   With dear ones I love the best—
Ere the pitcher at the fountain
   May in broken fragments lay,
Or the silver cord be loosened
   From the clasp of mortal clay.

Years ago, when we were younger,
   And the world was all untried,
How we loved to sit in council
   Over plans now set aside.

Now we linger close together—
  Nearer yet, each heart to heart—
Not with plans, but benedictions,
  Ere the time has come to part.

Oh, the parting, who could bear it?
  But for light beyond the grave—
Light that Jesus brought from Heaven,
  When he came the world to save.
Precious hope of sweet reunion
  With the loved ones here and there,
How it gilds our human sorrow
  With a joy like answered prayer.

One by one our friends have parted,
  Few remain of all we knew
In the homes of early childhood,
  When the world seemed bright and new.
But we fondly hope to meet them
  In the mansions of the blest,
"Where the wicked cease from troubling
  And the weary are at rest."

Yes, my dear, 1 know you'll miss me,
  I have been so long thy care;
At the hearthstone and the table
  There will be a vacant chair,
And at evening, when you gather
  Close around the mercy seat,

God will know how much you miss me,
   And will make His presence sweet.

But I would not have you carry
   Sorrow with you day by day;
God is love, and Heaven before you,
   While the Spirit guides the way.
Other dear ones yet are with you,
   Needing still your cheerful sway;
Let the sunshine of your presence
   Gladden still life's toilsome way.

When new trials overtake you,
   And life's cares press sore and keen,
And the world seems sad and lonely,
   With no one on whom to lean,
Then look up and lean on Jesus,
   Who has promised in His Word
Many precious, special blessings,
   For such hearts so deeply stirred.

When with me these scenes are ended,
   Fold my hands upon my breast;
Let the Elders be my bearers,
   Softly to my lowly rest.
Jesus sweetened earth and Heaven,
   And the tomb through which He passed,
And the soul that sleeps in Jesus
   Shall behold His face at last.

Let there be no showy pageant
  In consigning dust to dust;
Let my casket be the plainest —
  All alike will fade and rust.
I would have no costly marble
  Tell the world that I was dead,
While the dear ones left behind me
  Toiled in pain for daily bread.

In your heart you still may cherish
  All that's worthy of its trust,
But my failings—let them perish
  With the part beneath the dust.
At the morning of the rising,
  Soul and body to unite,
Not one trace of sin or weakness
  Then shall mar the vision bright.

One sweet thought I bid you cherish
  In fond memory's sacred shrine,
I could never fail to treasure
  All thy worth to me and mine.
All along life's checkered pathway
  Thou hast been my faithful dear;
God has often heard me say it
  When no ear but His could hear.

Life to us has been a battle—
  Fearful odds against us, too —

Weakness, sickness, partial blindness,
    With disasters not a few.
But the Lord has been our Keeper
    Through each dark and stormy night—
Never night so long and dreary
    But it had its dawning light.

So it will be in the morning,
    When the clouds have passed away;
Doubt and darkness lost forever
    In that bright, eternal day.
Holy Father, safely guide us
    By Thy strong, unerring hand,
One united, happy family,
    In Thy presence thus to stand.

9 7 8 3 7 4 4 6 5 2 2 7 8